Brrr! Where could you dive into the cold water of the world's largest lake?

The **continent** of North America!
A continent is a big piece of land.
There are seven continents on Earth.

Arctic Ocean

North
America

Atlantic
Ocean

Pacific
Ocean

South
America

Antarctica

NORTH AMERICA

by Madeline Donaldson

Lerner Publications Company • Minneapolis

Lerner Publications Company
A division of Lerner Publishing Group, Inc.
241 First Avenue North
Minneapolis, MN 55401 USA

For reading levels and more information, look up this title at www.lernerbooks.com.

Words in **bold type** are explained in a glossary on page 30.

Library of Congress Cataloging-in-Publication Data

Donaldson, Madeline.
    North America / by Madeline Donaldson.
      p.   cm. – (Pull ahead books)
    Summary: An introduction to some of the landmarks and characteristics of the continent of North America. Includes bibliographical references and index.
     ISBN-13: 978–0–8225–4722–8 (lib. bdg. : alk. paper)
     ISBN-10: 0–8225–4722–8 (lib. bdg. : alk. paper)
     1. North America–Juvenile literature. [1. North America.] I. Title. II. Series.
E38.5.D66 2005
917–dc22   2003016538

Manufactured in the United States of America
8 – CG – 11/1/13

Photo Acknowledgments

Photographs are used with the permission of: © Layne Kennedy/CORBIS, p. 3; © Robert Fried Photography, pp. 7, 9, 13, 21; © Michael Evans/The Image Finders, p. 8; © Robert Holmes/CORBIS, p. 10; © Werner Lobert/The Image Finders, p. 12; © Jeff Greenberg/Visuals Unlimited, pp. 14, 24; © Royalty-Free/CORBIS, p. 15; © Ann B. Swengel/Visuals Unlimited, p. 16; © Gary W. Carter/Visuals Unlimited, p. 17; © Shannon Liddell/Point of View Photography, p. 18; © Jack Ballard/Visuals Unlimited, p. 19; © Kennan Ward, p. 20; © Randy Faris/CORBIS, pp. 22–23; © Tourism Toronto, p. 25; © The Image Finders, pp. 26–27. Maps on pp. 4–5, 6, 11, and 29 by Laura Westlund.

The three big **countries** in North
America are Canada, the United
States, and Mexico.

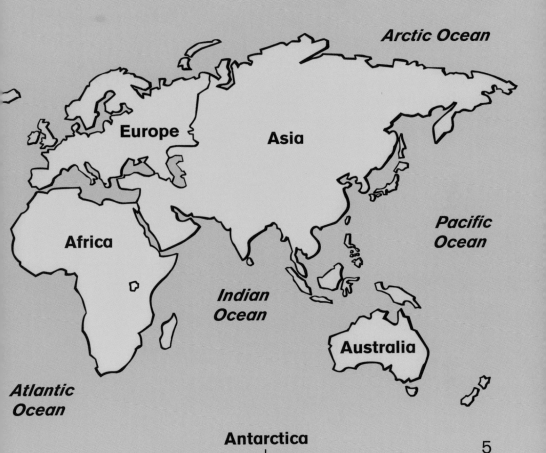

Arctic Ocean

Europe

Asia

Africa

Pacific
Ocean

Indian
Ocean

Australia

Atlantic
Ocean

Antarctica

NORTH AMERICA

Belize

Honduras

Nicaragua

Guatemala

El Salvador

Panama

Costa Rica

SOUTH AMERICA

Seven smaller countries link North America to South America.

Many **islands** are also part of North America. People enjoy playing on island beaches.

Whoosh! Oceans surround North America on three sides.

North America has many large and
small rivers. The longest is the
Mississippi River.

North America also has many large and small lakes. Remember the largest lake? It is called Lake Superior.

Lake Superior is one of the five Great Lakes. Most of them sit between Canada and the United States.

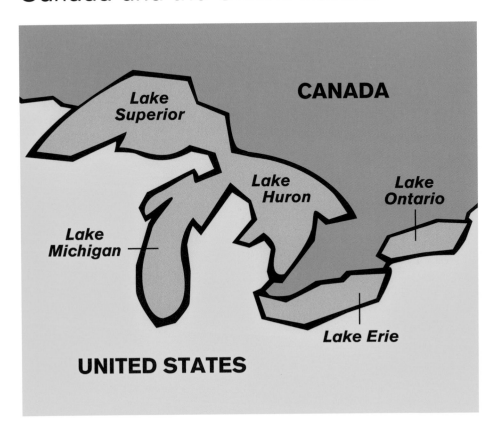

Long **chains** of mountains snake through North America. The continent's tallest mountain is Mount McKinley.

The Rocky Mountains go from Canada through the United States into Mexico.

Whew! North America also has hot,
dry **deserts.**

Other parts of North America are hot and wet. In Mexico's **tropical rain forests,** it rains all year long.

The Great **Plains** make up a huge area of grasslands. The plains lie in central North America.

Some plains are used for farmland. Farmland is also found in other parts of North America.

Many plants grow in North America.
Redwood trees are the tallest in the world.
They grow in western North America.

Prairie grasses cover the Great Plains.
The grasses give small animals places
to live.

Many other animals are able to live in North America. Polar bears stay in the coldest parts of the continent.

Colorful birds live in the tropical rain forests.

More than 450 million people live in all the parts of North America. Most people live in cities.

Mexico City is the **capital** of Mexico.
It is also North America's largest city.

Honk, honk! New York City is the
biggest city in the United States. It lies
in the eastern United States.

Canada's biggest city is Toronto. It sits on the shores of Lake Ontario.

North America has many interesting parts!
Do you know about Niagara Falls?

They crash down more than one hundred
feet in eastern North America.

There's always something new to learn about North America!

Cool Facts about North America

- North America covers more than 9 million square miles (24 million square km).

- Greenland is the largest island in North America. Other islands include Puerto Rico, Cuba, and Jamaica.

- The main rivers of North America are the Mississippi River, the Missouri River, the Ohio River, the Mackenzie River, the Colorado River, and the Rio Grande.

- The animals of North America include alligators, Canada geese, coyotes, porcupines, and polar bears.

- Prairie grasses and saguaro cactuses are two kinds of plants that grow in North America.

- The large cities of North America include Los Angeles, Chicago, Mexico City, New York City, Toronto, Vancouver, Montreal, and Washington, D.C.

- Most North Americans speak English, Spanish, or French.

Map of North America

Greenland
(Denmark)

Alaska
(U.S.)

Canada

United
States

Caribbean
Islands

Mexico

Belize

Guatemala

El Salvador

Honduras

Nicaragua

Panama

Costa Rica

Glossary

capital: a city where a government is based

chains: series of linked things. A mountain chain usually makes a long, thick line on a map.

continent: one of seven big pieces of land on Earth

countries: places with their own government and borders (or edges)

deserts: hot areas that don't get much rain

islands: pieces of land surrounded by water

plains: a large area of grassland

tropical rain forests: rich green forests that get a lot of rain throughout the year

Further Reading and Websites

Foster, Leila Merrell. *North America.* Crystal Lake, IL: Heinemann Library, 2001.

Fowler, Allan. *North America.* Danbury, CT: Children's Press, 2001.

Hamilton, Janice. *Canada.* Minneapolis: Carolrhoda Books, Inc., 1999.

Nelson, Robin. *Where Is My Continent?* Minneapolis: Lerner Publications Company, 2002.

Raczek, Linda Theresa. *Stories from Native North America.* Crystal Lake, IL: Raintree/Steck Vaughn, 2000.

Sayre, April Pulley. *Welcome to North America!* Brookfield, CT: Millbrook Press, 2003.

Schnetzler, Pattie. *Widdermaker.* Minneapolis: Carolrhoda Books, Inc., 2002.

Streissguth, Tom. *Mexico.* Minneapolis: Carolrhoda Books, Inc., 1997.

Enchanted Learning

http://enchantedlearning.com/geography/namer/

The geography section of this website has links to every continent.

North America–National Zoo

http://natzoo.si.edu/Animals/NorthAmerica/ForKids/

This site offers puzzles, games, pictures, and information on many of the animals in North America.

Index